Extreme
Weather

Science Tackles
Global Warming
and Climate Change

SWIMMING
PROHIBITED

GCC

Due to low water level
all boating

PROHIBITED
UNTIL FURTHER NOTICE

By order of General Manager
Goulburn City Council

Extreme
Weather

Science Tackles Global Warming and Climate Change

By Kathleen Simpson

Dr. Jonathan D. W. Kahl, Consultant

NATIONAL
GEOGRAPHIC
Washington, DC

Contents

< Flood waters resulting from severe rainstorms in Snohomish, Washington, surround a house in November 2006.

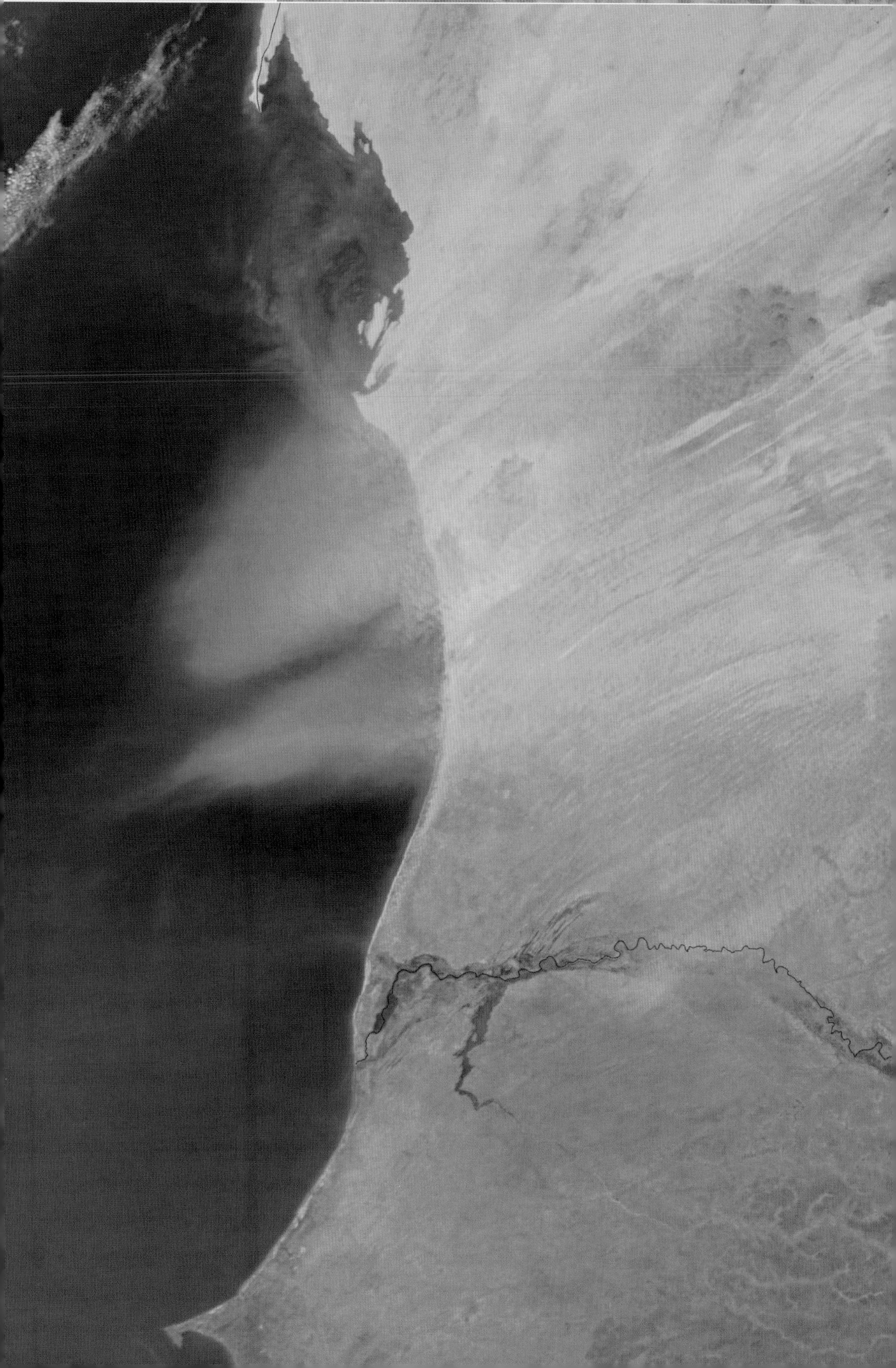

< An aerial photograph of the Atlantic Ocean shows a large cloud of sand and dust blowing over from the Sahara Desert.

T he atmosphere is an exciting place. Its brilliant rainbows and sunset colors have inspired artists for centuries. Its swirling winds produce devastating tornadoes and hurricanes, hailstones the size of grapefruit, and recently dumped nearly two feet of snow on my home state of Wisconsin.

The atmosphere is mysterious. We know that daytime is warmer than nighttime and that summer is warmer than winter, yet we cannot accurately predict weather more than one week into the future. Lightning strikes more than three million times every day, yet meteorologists still cannot predict exactly where a flash will occur.

What happens to the atmosphere when we load it up with dust from the Sahara desert? Does pollution warm or cool the climate? Will global warming produce more El Niños or stronger hurricanes? Scientists studying the atmosphere use many different types of clues, such as ancient air bubbles trapped in Antarctic ice and buildings abandoned by ancient civilizations, to study how climate has changed in the past. Other scientists combine this information with computer models to predict how climate may change in the future.

This book describes some of the fascinating ways that scientists are studying weather and climate change. Enjoy this book and our exciting, mysterious atmosphere!

– Jonathan Kahl
Milwaukee, 2008

Λ **Jonathan Kahl examines the aerodynamic properties of snow in Wisconsin.**

Map of Extreme Weather Around the World

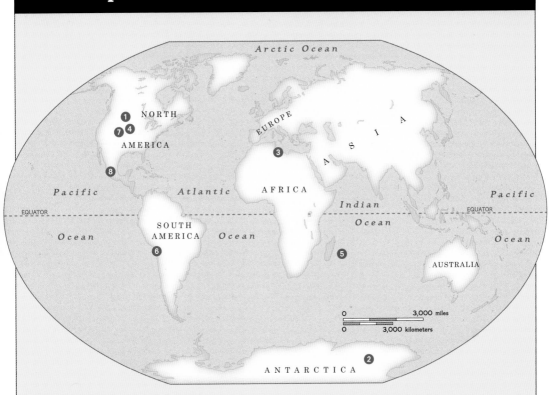

1 A rancher in Fort Keogh, Montana found a snowflake 15 inches wide and 8 inches thick (38 cm wide by 20 cm thick) on January 28, 1887. That's wider than a dinner plate!

2 Vostock Station, Antarctica recorded the coldest temperature ever measured anywhere on Earth. In July of 1983, Vostok Station's thermometer read 128.6 degrees below zero (-89.2 C).

3 The hottest temperature ever recorded was in El Aziziya, Libya, on September 13, 1922. It was 136 degrees Fahrenheit (57.8 C).

4 The largest hailstone ever recorded fell in Aurora, Nebraska on June 22, 2003. It measured seven inches (almost 8 cm) across—almost the size of a bowling ball!

5 Six feet (1.8 m) of rain fell in 24 hours in a place called La Reunion Island (in the Indian Ocean, a few hundred miles east of Madagascar). That's a record for 24-hour rainfall! It happened on January 7-8, 1966.

6 For 14 years, not a drop of rain fell on Arica Desert, Chile, the driest spot in the world.

7 In 24 hours, April 14-15, 1921, more than 75 feet (almost 23 m) of snow fell on Silver Lake, Colorado—enough snow to bury a truck!

8 Snow fell in Guadalajara, Mexico in December of 1997—the first time in 120 years.

> **La Reunion Island**

9

TIMELINE OF
Historical Weather Events

∧ **1900** · Survivors of the Galveston Hurricane, which hit Galveston, Texas, in 1900, sift through the wreckage. More lives were lost in this natural disaster than in any other hurricane in U.S. history.

1870	1910	1930	1970

1870s

Greenhouse gas production jumps as factories, farms, and railroads boom in the Industrial Revolution begun in 1800.

1900

Massive hurricane swamps Galveston Island.

1913

Swedish scientist Svente Arrhenius is the first to predict a rise in atmospheric temperature due to increasing levels of carbon dioxide.

1930

Dust Bowl drought strikes the southern Great Plains.

Experts point out that Earth is clearly getting warmer.

1972

Greenland ice cores show sudden (occurring in less than a decade) climate changes in the last 11,000 years.

1970

The first Earth Day brings widespread attention to the planet's fragile nature.

< The first Earth Day, celebrated on April 22, 1970, in Chicago, Illinois, drew marchers wearing gas masks to protest air pollution, including the increase in greenhouse gases in the environment.

∧ 2006 · One of the largest icebergs ever recorded— 170 miles (273 km) long and 25 miles (40 km) wide— broke off the seaward edge of the Ross Ice Shelf in March 2000. Most scientists blame global warming for the increasing rate at which the Shelf is melting.

< 1997 · An El Niño effect in 1997 and 1998 produced drought conditions throughout the already arid region of Indonesia.

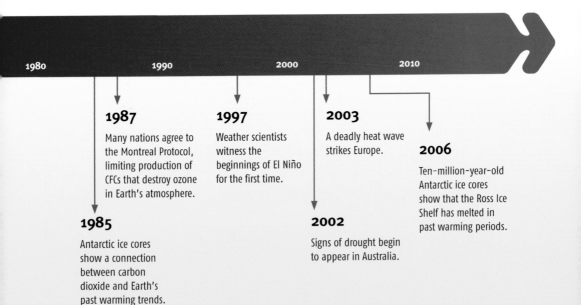

1980   1990   2000   2010

1987

Many nations agree to the Montreal Protocol, limiting production of CFCs that destroy ozone in Earth's atmosphere.

1985

Antarctic ice cores show a connection between carbon dioxide and Earth's past warming trends.

1997

Weather scientists witness the beginnings of El Niño for the first time.

2002

Signs of drought begin to appear in Australia.

2003

A deadly heat wave strikes Europe.

2006

Ten-million-year-old Antarctic ice cores show that the Ross Ice Shelf has melted in past warming periods.

Clues From the Past

CHAPTER 1

Hot Debate Over Global Warming

On the rocky islands of California's Farallon National Wildlife Refuge, seawater crashes against a wild and empty shoreline. Over the ocean's roar, scientists listen for cries of seabirds searching for food in the churning water. The islands are littered with nests of birds that come here each spring to breed and feast on krill, tiny sea animals. This year is eerily different. Most of the birds have come, laid their eggs, and then vanished, leaving chicks and eggs behind. The reason: not enough krill to go around. Scientists think global warming may have caused krill-rich ocean currents to change,

< Seagulls nest among the rocks and dunes at the Farallon National Wildlife Refuge, a group of islands west of San Francisco, California, where up to 250,000 birds breed each year. In addition to seabirds, the islands are home to seals and sea lions.

leaving hundreds of thousands of island birds to go elsewhere or starve.

On the opposite side of the planet, another group of islanders abandon their homes. In the island nation of Kiribati, waves roll higher each year onto sandy beaches, swamping shorelines, farms, and homes. Like the birds of the Farallons, Kiribati's people are leaving their islands behind. The country's president, Anote Tong, believes his nation will be the first to disappear because of global warming. He has told the world that the rising ocean will wash over Kiribati by the middle of this century—in *your* lifetime. Other island nations will disappear the same way, say scientists, unless world leaders work together to slow global warming.

Whenever the subject of global warming comes up, hot debate is sure to follow. Many scientists feel frustrated with slow-acting leaders in large countries like China and the United States. Others believe that while Earth is growing warmer, this is a natural event on a constantly changing planet. They're unsure if we can or should try to stop it. Still other scientists think that quick action would be too expensive and that more research is needed to develop less expensive, cost-effective solutions. One point scientists, environmentalists, politicians, and the public agree upon, however, is the need to learn more about climate change.

V **Within the next 50 years, higher sea levels due to global warming will mean the end of the island nation of Kiribati, shown here, as it is engulfed by water.**

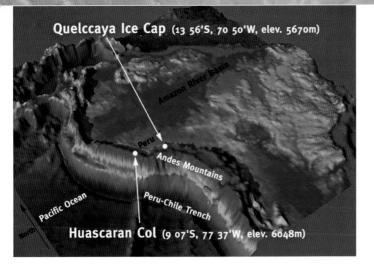

Quelccaya Ice Cap (13 56'S, 70 50'W, elev. 5670m)

Amazon River Basin

Peru

Andes Mountains

Pacific Ocean

Peru-Chile Trench

North

Huascaran Col (9 07'S, 77 37'W, elev. 6048m)

∧ The Andes Mountains of Peru are home to the Quelccaya Ice Cap, the largest ice cap located in a tropical region. In late 2007, the temperatures recorded were the highest in the last few decades.

Extreme Expeditions Hunt for Clues in Ice

The wind is fierce on the high slopes of Peru's tallest mountain, Huascarán, and it is cold enough to freeze tears on a mountain climber's eyelashes. In the thin air, climbers struggle for breath, as avalanches, crevasses (deep, wide cracks in the ice), and powerful windstorms make the job even harder. A team of scientists from the U.S., under the leadership of Dr. Lonnie Thompson, have traveled to this ruthless place to collect ice samples.

Dr. Thompson's crew are carrying several tons of gear in their packs along with heavy drilling equipment stowed on the backs of horses and mules. Local people guide them to a spot where they set up camp on a glacier—a permanently frozen mass of very slowly sliding ice.

The scientists set up their solar-powered drill and bring up large tubes of ice called "cores." Each core is made up of bands, or layers, of ice that an expert can read like pages in a book. The bands of ice were formed at different times over many years, so that the bottom bands are older than the top ones. Each band indicates the climate conditions at the time. Weather scientists known as paleoclimatologists can distinguish warm periods from cold ones, and dry periods from wet ones by "reading" the bands. Some glacial cores hold ice that is tens of thousands of years old.

> The edge of the Quelccaya Ice Cap falls off into a spectacular ice cliff 180 feet (55 meters) high.

15

Drilling Through Antarctic Ice

In late 2006, during Antarctica's summer, scientists from Italy, the U.S., Germany, and New Zealand drilled through an enormous sheet of ice known as the Ross Ice Shelf. The ice shelf is attached to land, but floats in the Ross Sea. In some places it is 3,000 feet (915 m) thick. These scientists cut through the ice shelf and into the seabed below, bringing up cores of ten-million-year-old sediment.

Once back at their research station, the scientists sliced into the cores and were surprised by what they found. A large number of tiny fossilized creatures called diatoms pointed to periods when the Ross Sea was open water. The vast Ross Ice Shelf, a body of ice the size of France, must have melted and refrozen over and over through time. What changes must have taken place in Earth's climate to cause the ice shelf to melt and refreeze?

∧ Scientists in Antarctica monitor a solar-powered drill that will bring up ice cores from which they can obtain information on climate change over the years.

After several weeks on the mountain, the scientists begin the difficult task of getting the ice cores home. They pack the cores in special containers to keep them frozen on the long trek down the mountain. Traveling back to the U.S., the researchers make sure the cores aren't misplaced in busy airports, where they might melt. Once back in the laboratory, the scientists are finally able to open the containers and slice into the ice to study it. The history of the climate changes in this region will soon be revealed.

A Changing Earth

Ice cores tell us that Earth's climate has changed many times, from warm, fertile periods to ice ages and back again. These changes weren't seasonal, from winter to spring to summer—they were long-term, some lasting hundreds of thousands of years. In a few cases, climate change happened abruptly, possibly in as little as five years. What caused Earth's climate to flip from cold to hot or vice versa? It's still hard to say, but we do know that past fluctuations happened as a result of natural events, such as changes on the sun's surface.

V Smokestacks from a factory in Taiyan, China, pollute the air with gases that probably contribute to global warming. China is the second-largest producer of greenhouse gases in the world, but is likely to overtake the leader in emissions, the United States, in 2008.

Earth is in a warming period now. Most scientists agree that, this time, it's happening very fast, and not only because of changes in the sun. Chemicals in the air, called greenhouse gases, contribute to the changes.

V The streets of Beijing are crowded with cars and buses that contribute to China's growing emissions problem.

The Greenhouse Effect

Layers of gases, including greenhouse gases such as water vapor, carbon dioxide, methane, and nitrous oxide, surround Earth like a foil candy wrapper. This wrapper of gases is our atmosphere. Earth's atmosphere lets in sunlight and keeps warmth close to the planet's surface. This is known as the greenhouse effect. If the atmosphere were to disappear, Earth would be too cold for people to survive here. Too much greenhouse gas in the atmosphere, however, holds in too much heat, causing Earth to grow warmer.

Greenhouse gases do occur in nature, but people are adding to the natural greenhouse effect. Scientists think that pollution and the destruction of forests all contribute to global warming.

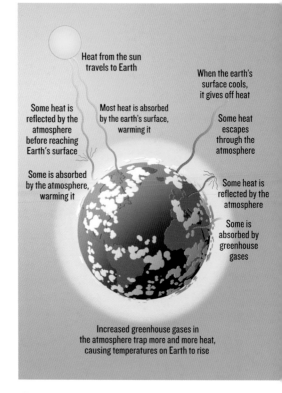

Heat from the sun travels to Earth

When the earth's surface cools, it gives off heat

Some heat is reflected by the atmosphere before reaching Earth's surface

Most heat is absorbed by the earth's surface, warming it

Some heat escapes through the atmosphere

Some is absorbed by the atmosphere, warming it

Some heat is reflected by the atmosphere

Some is absorbed by greenhouse gases

Increased greenhouse gases in the atmosphere trap more and more heat, causing temperatures on Earth to rise

⋀ **Energy from the sun warms Earth, creating an environment where we can survive.**

The Ozone Layer

You may have heard of a "hole" in part of Earth's atmosphere—the part often called the ozone layer. The ozone layer occurs in the stratosphere, Earth's upper atmosphere (the greenhouse effect and global warming occur in Earth's lower atmosphere). In the 1970s, scientists discovered that chemicals known as chlorofluorocarbons, or CFCs, were breaking up the ozone layer. CFCs were used in a variety of products, including aerosol sprays, refrigerants, and foams. This "hole" could have been disastrous, because the ozone layer shields us from the sun's harmful ultraviolet rays.

In 1987, countries around the world signed the Montreal Protocol, agreeing to drastically cut back on the production of CFCs. It will take many years for the CFCs in our stratosphere to break apart, and we now know that other kinds of pollution also make it hard for the ozone layer to heal itself. The Montreal Protocol is an example of successful international cooperation, and many people believe it is the example to follow for slowing the rate at which Earth is warming.

A Warmer World

Weather is what happens today, next week, and next month; climate is what we learn to expect over longer periods of time. What will happen to our weather as Earth's climate changes? This is a question scientists are trying to answer, and the need for answers is urgent.

Earth is already heating up—average temperatures are about 1°F (–0.6°C) warmer than they were a century ago. One degree may not sound like much, but it can make a big difference. Our oceans are heating up, too, and as water warms, it expands, causing ocean levels to rise. Melting polar ice also raises sea levels. Scientists wonder how warmer, higher oceans will affect our weather.

Much of Earth's glacial ice is melting, too. Peru's Quelccaya Ice Cap has lost more than one-fifth of its ice, just since Dr. Thompson's first visit in 1974. He predicts that twenty years from now, Quelccaya will be gone completely.

Will global warming bring more extreme weather? Although our oceans are expanding, water may become scarcer than it is now. To learn about drought and how Australian scientists explore caves to understand it, read Chapter 2. Read Chapter 3 to learn about El Niño and La Niña. These are warming and cooling patterns in the Pacific Ocean that drive storms and droughts around the world. To learn how warm water fuels storms—including hurricanes—and how high-tech storm-hunting aircraft help us study them, read Chapter 4. Chapter 5 discusses Saharan dust that may actually slow the growth of hurricanes and reduce global warming. To discover ways that you and your government can make a difference in Earth's future, read Chapter 6. The more we know, the better off we will be, whatever the future brings.

▽ **Dr. Lonnie Thompson (*left*), a glaciologist at Ohio State University, and University of Texas botanist Blanca Leon examine pieces of ancient moss that the retreating Quelccaya Ice Cap has left exposed.**

Learn About Drought

CHAPTER 2

Dry Times in Australia

T he Australian summer of 2005–2006 was a scorcher—the hottest on record in New South Wales. You might think the heat would send children dashing through sprinklers and leaping into the city pool. Not in the Australian town of Goulburn! The town was under Level 5 water restrictions—water hoses were banned completely, and the pool had been closed for months. Gardens turned brittle and brown, and dust settled over unwashed cars. People showered standing in buckets, so they could reuse the water somewhere else. The region had been living with drought since 2002, and water grew more precious every day.

< The receding water in the Pejar Dam in Goulburn, Australia, is monitored by Matthew O'Rourke, who reports that the dam is at less than 10 percent capacity, resulting in water restrictions for the town's 23,000 citizens.

Outside of town, sheep ranchers eyed the blue sky grimly, knowing their animals would not have enough to eat. They sold off some sheep, but had to buy feed for the rest—an expensive problem. Crops wilted and fruit trees died in Australia's "food bowl," an area known as the Murray-Darling Basin. As creeks, rivers, and lakes dried up, many farmers sold off land, because they couldn't grow anything without water.

With fields and forests so dry, wildfires (Australians call them bushfires) licked up whatever grass was left. Summer temperatures rose and a dry wind picked up—fires even threatened Sydney, the continent's largest city.

> A farmer in Goulburn, Australia, holds a dry, empty rain gauge. The town has been in the grip of a drought since 2002.

V Usually fertile farmland around Goulburn, 130 miles (210 kilometers) southwest of the capital city of Sydney, is parched, leaving little grass for sheep and cattle to graze upon.

Solving the Mystery of the Maya

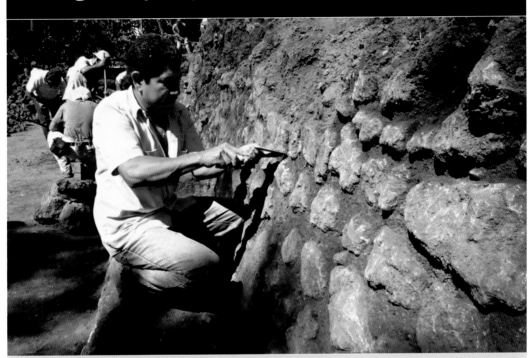

⋀ A scientist studies the Maya ruins at Tazumal in Chalchuapa, El Salvador, for information on climate change that might have led to the downfall of the once great society.

About 1,200 years ago, a mighty empire thrived in the jungles of what is now Mexico. Great, square pyramids rose above bustling cities where artists, astronomers, and mathematicians worked. Fertile farms fed the millions of people who made the Maya Empire function.

Then, around A.D. 900, the Maya left their cities behind. They abandoned their farms, let buildings and pyramids fall into ruin, and a great civilization crumbled. For a long time, scientists scratched their heads and asked each other why.

Paleoclimatologists have found clues to solve the mystery of what happened to the Maya. Sediment cores from lakes show that the Maya suffered three terrible droughts between A.D. 810 and 910. The cores also show that, around the same time, trees became scarce. A lack of trees would have made the air hotter, so that water would have evaporated more quickly, making the droughts worse. Did the Maya burn or cut down the trees? It's possible; even today, many Central American farmers burn forest to make room for crops.

Science shows that Maya cities probably emptied because the people were starving. They suffered years of terrible drought and probably put too much stress on the land by overcrowding and cutting down trees. The question is: can modern people learn from the Maya people's mistakes?

Searching in Caves for Answers

Drought is no stranger to Australia— it's the world's driest inhabited continent. To explore its long history of drought, scientists go underground, into the Wombeyan cave system. Damp-skinned geckos watch as Dr. Janece McDonald and her team squeeze through the cave's tight opening. Climbing, crawling, and dropping from ledges, they make their way to the research site. The caves are cool and dark, except for light from headlamps, and the only sounds are dripping water, low voices, and the chuff-chuff of clothing against rock. Upon reaching the site, the scientists set up equipment they've packed in with them and get to work.

Using active stalactites and stalagmites, scientists from the University of Newcastle are building a thousand-year record of drought and flood in the area. Such a record will help scientists understand drought patterns and forecast possible effects of global warming.

Here's how it works: as rainwater seeps through soil and limestone, it collects minerals, especially calcite. Trickling through tiny cracks, the water drips into caves. As the water evaporates, it leaves behind traces of calcite and other minerals—a sort of mineral "footprint." Over time, the calcite builds up, forming long, pale stalactites hanging from the ceiling and stalagmites rising from the floor

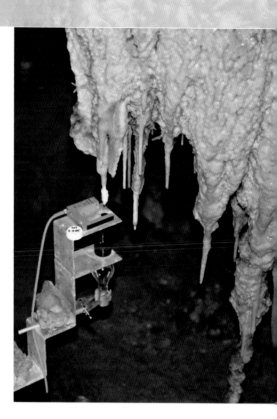

∧ Dr. Janece McDonald studies stalactites at the Wombeyan Caves in New South Wales, Australia, in order to chart the history of a thousand years of climate changes and to learn more about drought.

below. By analyzing minerals in these formations, scientists work out the age of caves and can piece together rainfall patterns from the past.

The weather outside may be blistering hot, but in the cave, scientists work in quiet comfort. They're careful not to disturb their surroundings, respectful of a fragile environment. The stalagmite records they find are detailed enough to show rainfall changes from one year to the next or even from one season to the next. Cave formations could reveal ancient climate secrets, too, possibly going all the way back to the last time Earth was warmer than it is now. Such records could be especially important, because they might tell us what the current global warming will bring. Will Australia experience even longer droughts? Will droughts be interrupted by periods of heavy rain?

The Dust Bowl

Scientists will tell you that drought is what happens when an area receives less precipitation than usual. It's a natural event that has always occurred, and it occurs almost everywhere. Two extreme droughts struck the U.S. in the 20th century: the 1930s Dust Bowl and a second drought in the 1950s.

In the early 20th century, thousands of families settled the Great Plains region of the U.S., plowing up grass and planting mile after mile of wheat. This turned out to be a costly mistake—those native grasses had held dry soil in place during regular droughts. When ranchers brought in large herds of cattle to eat whatever grass was left and grind up the soil with their hooves, the delicately balanced ecosystem was further disrupted.

Drought slammed the Great Plains in the early 1930s, and the wheat plants were unable to keep the dry soil in place. Windstorms picked it up by the ton, sometimes blowing dust all the way to the Atlantic Ocean. Brown clouds

▼ A dust storm approaches the town of Stratford, Texas, in 1935, on a day that was called "Black Sunday" because the dust clouds blocked all light from the sun. Some residents of the town were suffocated by the dust clouds.

steamrollered across farms and towns, and dust piled up around buildings. People had to shovel it away like snow. It filled eyes, noses, and lungs, making people and animals sick; it destroyed farm machinery. Thousands of people moved away from the Dust Bowl of the Great Plains, looking for work elsewhere.

In 1935, government agents stepped in to help, showing farmers how to plant different crops from one year to the next, to keep the soil healthy. The government workers planted rows of trees to break the wind and bought cattle from ranchers who couldn't afford feed. In the late 1930s, the drought finally ended, but some farmers soon forgot the lessons they had learned about taking care of the land. When drought struck again a few decades later, dust storms returned.

∧ A farmhouse is buried by dust from a severe storm. Scenes like this were common throughout the 1930s as faulty farming practices rid the Great Plains of native grasses.

Desertification

∧ Starving cattle search for food in the drought-stricken Sahel region in Senegal. Thirty years of drought have led to a nationwide famine.

When drought strikes on the edge of a desert, it can trigger even bigger problems. Fifty years ago, tall grass covered most of the African Sahel, a wide area of land that is wedged between the Sahara Desert and more fertile lands on the opposite side. In the late 1960s, the region fell into a long drought. Rivers and lakes no longer held enough water for a growing population. Hungry farm animals grazed heavily and packed the soil so hard that it no longer held water. Trees and grass in the Sahel disappeared, and soil blew away on the wind. Some parts of the Sahel blended with the neighboring Sahara. This process, known as desertification, occurs around the world, and it's hard to stop. Today, the Sahel remains a damaged environment, but experts believe that careful grazing, irrigation, and tree planting could save the land.

∧ An irrigation line in western China brings water to a young forest that the Chinese hope will provide protection against increasing desertification in this dust bowl region.

Easing the Effects of Drought

In August 2007, rain began to pour down on Goulburn, Australia, and town leaders loosened water restrictions. Whether or not the rain will be enough to end the worst drought in the nation's history remains to be seen. But, already the once brown landscape has turned green and fertile farmland has returned to the region. Farmers are able to graze their sheep and cattle locally. Residents of Goulburn, winner of a national award for water conservation, remain cautious. Although the local dam's capacity returned to 54%, locals still use recycled or "gray" water to irrigate their gardens, utilize rainwater tanks, and continue to pursue technologies to cope with dry conditions. We do know that drought will return.

Scientists say a hotter Earth will mean more droughts for places like Australia. As residents of a warming planet, we can take steps to ease the effects of drought. We can leave native plants and trees in place, irrigate only when needed, and take measures to protect the soil. We can avoid moving into places where there are already more people than local rivers and lakes can support. We can turn off the water while we brush our teeth, and we can run the dishwasher only when it's full. In other words, we can learn to use water wisely.

El Niño and La Niña

CHAPTER 3

Warm Oceans Drive Weird Weather

The 1997 weather pattern known as El Niño struck first in South America, where skies opened up and dumped rain. Rivers in Peru and Ecuador swelled, washing away farmhouses, crops, and livestock, while families scrambled for higher ground. Low-lying land that had been dry for more than a decade filled up with the rivers' overflow, making lakes where there were none before.

On the other side of the Pacific, Indonesian farmers burned off fields in their usual way, expecting the rainy season to put out fires. But El Niño held back the rains, and the region fell into drought.

< El Niño has an effect on weather throughout the world. In Clear Oaks, California, flooding caused by the weather pattern in February 1998 reached its highest levels since 1914.

Fires burned unchecked, flames spread to rain forests, and blinding clouds of smoke lay over Indonesia.

Wild weather struck the U.S., too. One evening in February, low-hanging storm clouds swept into Florida from the Gulf of Mexico. Flashes of lightning burned up the sky, thunder rattled windows, and tornadoes tore across the state.

For the first time in more than a century, snow fell in Guadalajara, Mexico.

In the Atlantic Ocean, wind currents blasted apart storms that, in a normal year, might have become hurricanes.

The violent weather in Peru was part of a pattern familiar to farmers and fishers there. For centuries, they've spoken of El Niño—an event that happens every few years, when Pacific waters warm up and months of flooding rains follow. Because it peaks around Christmastime, the fishers named the event after the child Jesus. *El Niño* means "The Boy" in Spanish.

∧ The remains of a rain forest on the island of Borneo smolder after being cleared by fire. Fewer trees in the environment have led to warmer temperatures, changing weather patterns around the world.

∧∧ A tornado touches down along a street in Galveston, Texas, in June 1997.

What Are El Niño and La Niña?

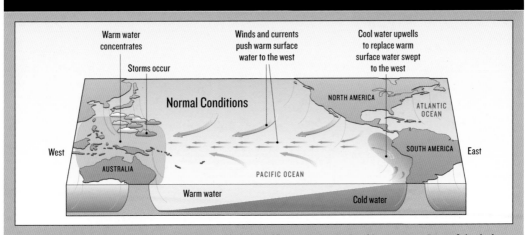

In most years, sunlight warms the surface of the Pacific Ocean near Earth's equator. Powerful winds blow west, pushing the warm water away from the Americas. Cool water surges up from the depths to replace water that has moved west. Meanwhile, on the western edge of the Pacific, moisture rises off the warm ocean. This warm, rising air feeds storms, and countries on that side of the ocean get rain.

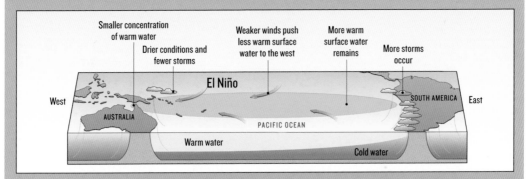

In an El Niño year, winds over the Pacific are too weak to blow warm surface water away from the Americas. A long, warm pool stretches across the ocean, and moisture rises off it, feeding storms in the Americas. Countries on the Pacific's western edge stay drier than usual. One weather event triggers another, causing a chain reaction around the world.

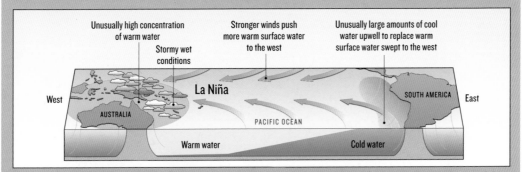

In the year after El Niño, the weather pattern sometimes reverses itself. Pacific winds are more powerful than usual, pushing warm water into a knot on the western edge of the ocean. Weather is just as extreme as it was the year before, but opposite; places that had drenching rain now have drought. Places that had drought now have floods and mud slides. This reverse pattern is called La Niña.

Learning the Rhythms of El Niño

Paleoclimatologists pore over tree rings, corals, sediments, and ice cores, looking for clues to El Niño's rhythms. Those rhythms have changed over time. El Niño occurs more often and lasts longer than it did a hundred years ago. We expect it to happen every three to seven years, but the ten years between 1997 and 2007 brought four El Niños. Is this change because of global warming? Scientists would like to find out.

The Great Flood of 2006

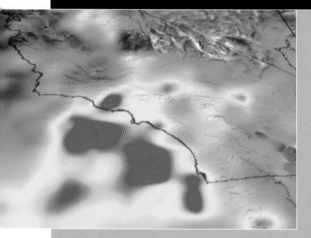

∧ The "pineapple express" moves in toward San Diego, California, from Hawaii, bringing increasingly heavy amounts of rain, illustrated in red on this NASA weather image. Over 8 inches (20 cm) of rain fell in the red-shaded areas.

The "pineapple express"—that's what meteorologists call powerful winds that carry warm, moist air across the Pacific Ocean to the northwestern coast of the U.S. These rain-packed winds are especially dangerous during weak El Niño winters, like the winter of 2006-07. It was the pineapple express that carried tropical air to the Washington coast in November 2006. Day upon day of record-setting rain pounded the state. Floodwaters gouged out riverbanks across the region. Pavement crumbled into car-sized chunks under the relentless pounding of fast-moving water. The landscape of Mount Rainier National Park was forever changed as angry rivers cut new tracks through the forest.

Levees broke, making lakes out of farms. Hikers and elk hunters found themselves cut off by rising water as searchers in helicopters roamed the skies looking for them. Several drivers, ignoring "road closed" signs, drove into high water, only to be swept away in their vehicles. Some drowned; others eventually found rescue.

As government leaders ordered city after city to evacuate, rescue crews boarded aircraft to help those trapped by rising water. Helicopters plucked stranded people off rooftops and out of vehicles. Closed schools became shelters for flood victims who had nowhere else to go. Water and sewage plants shut down, and ironically, government leaders had to bring in drinking water from drier areas.

When the rain tapered off, Washington's rivers crested and slowed. Residents paddled boats out to see what remained of their homes after "the great flood of 2006." Meanwhile, meteorologists scanned computer screens nervously, knowing that more rain could be coming soon.

Months before the 1997 storms hit Peru, scientists at the U.S. National Oceanographic and Atmospheric Administration (NOAA) were jabbing fingers at computer screens and talking excitedly about El Niño. They double- and triple-checked numbers as water temperatures in the tropical Pacific rose. How did meteorologists in Seattle know the tropical Pacific water was heating up? They relied on measurements taken by weather buoys put in place just a few years before. The buoys, dotting the Pacific from Central America to Hawaii, told them that El Niño was on its way. It was the first time in history that scientists were able to warn people about El Niño before the wild weather started.

Today, scientists around the world count on those buoys, part of an international program known as the TAO/Triton array. Weather buoys are tough, floating weather stations, tied to the deep sea floor by long cables and chains. Using high-tech instruments to measure water temperature and wind speed and direction, they send information to communication satellites so that data can be relayed to research laboratories.

∨ A scientist takes measurements from a weather buoy located in the Pacific Ocean in 2005.

calculator to do the same trillion problems, it would take you about 80 million years! Scientists can now forecast some El Niño effects a year in advance, saving lives and billions of dollars.

∧ The Topex/Poseidon satellite was launched in 1992 to map the ocean's surface.

The satellites relay those measurements to scientists, but that's not all they do. French/U.S. satellite Topex/Poseidon also measures water levels in the world's oceans; the measurements are accurate down to a couple of inches (4 to 5 cm). Ocean levels are important because as water warms, it expands, and sea levels rise; higher sea levels can mean El Niño is heating up.

As measurements pour in, scientists use supercomputers to make sense of all the data. These machines work trillions of problems every second. If you tried to use a

Making History

El Niño and La Niña are more than weather-makers; they make history:

■ Without El Niño, Spanish conqueror Francisco Pizarro might never have defeated the great Inca empire of Peru. In 1532, El Niño drenched the desert, providing much-needed water and vegetation for the Spanish army's march to the Inca capital.

■ Savage weather held up the Lewis and Clark expedition for weeks as the explorers crossed Oregon in 1804–05, an El Niño year.

■ In the winter of 1812, La Niña set up early snow and bitterly cold conditions for Europe. French ruler Napoleon Bonaparte chose this unfortunate time to invade Russia. Harsh weather killed thousands of his soldiers, and Napoleon was forced to retreat.

■ In 1875, La Niña brought drought and a plague of locusts to the western United States. Witnesses say the locusts looked like glittering clouds, filling the sky and covering every surface. They ate crops, grass, and even each other, driving some farming families to leave for good.

El Niño Every Year?

How does global warming affect El Niño and La Niña? It's a puzzling question: many scientists say global warming causes a hotter "background" of weather, and El Niño warms oceans on top of that. The high number of El Niños we've seen in recent years (with few La Niñas) makes this theory seem likely. If it is true, we could see El Niño-like weather nearly every year—mild winters for the northern U.S., heavy thunderstorms and flooding for the Gulf Coast and California. Other scientists suggest that natural El Niño cycles, having little to do with global warming, are at work. Either way, keeping an eye on El Niño is becoming more important all the time.

∧ In November 2001, Hurricane Michelle destroyed homes and crops in the island nation of Cuba. The city of Havana, shown here, was battered by waves 25 feet (8 m) high.

Hurricane!

CHAPTER 4

Storm Hunters at Work

After hours of flying, NOAA's storm-hunting jet has finally reached the hurricane. Heavy rain lashes the aircraft, and hurricane winds toss it around. The crew tries to hang on and work at the same time, busily checking instruments and taking measurements.

Later, as the jet enters the eye of the storm, the turbulence suddenly stops, and the crew gazes up at clear, blue sky. Below, the ocean churns, with waves as high as a two-story house. Says meteorologist Robert Rogers, "[Seeing the eye up close] gives you a tremendous appreciation of the power of these storms, and it leaves you even more determined to better understand and predict them."

< This photograph of the eye of Hurricane Helene was taken by a crew member of the space shuttle *Atlantis* in September 2006.

Anatomy of a Hurricane

Along with winds blowing faster than a car moving at highway speed, hurricanes often produce torrential rain, tornadoes, lightning, and, deadliest of all, storm surge. Storm surge is a great rush of seawater that rolls ashore with the storm, sometimes sweeping away cars, knocking down buildings, and flooding towns.

Hurricane wind, clouds, and rain move in bands around a nearly circular eye. Inside the eye, usually about 20 miles (32 km) across, weather is fairly calm, but just outside is the eyewall, where wind and rain are most intense.

Warm water gives life to hurricanes—over cool oceans or land, the storms weaken or fall apart. A warm ocean isn't the only necessary ingredient, though. For a storm to turn into a hurricane, water temperature, wind direction, moisture, and nearness to Earth's equator all must be exactly right. If they are, a storm might become a hurricane—maybe. Weather scientists like Robert Rogers want to know how and why some storms become hurricanes. Having that information would enable them to forecast more accurately where the storms will go and how powerful they'll become.

Scientists would also like to know how global warming affects hurricanes. Since the early 1990s, we've seen more Atlantic hurricanes, and many scientists think Earth's warming oceans may be causing the increase. But in the past, we've cycled through 20- or 30-year periods of frequent storms, followed by 20 or 30 years with few hurricanes. It's possible that we're seeing that cycle again now.

V Hurricane Michelle, which hit Cuba in 2001, brought high winds and torrential rains, making evacuation difficult for many residents.

Hurricanes No One Will Forget

Hurricane Katrina, which pounded the Gulf Coast of the United States in 2005, was the costliest storm in the nation's history, causing hundreds of billions of dollars in damages. Two years later, Katrina-related expenses continue to pile up. As horrific as it was, Katrina was not the deadliest storm; the Galveston Hurricane of 1900 was worse, killing between 8,000 and 10,000 people. The most powerful hurricane to hit the U.S. mainland was probably Camille, if "power" is measured by wind speed. On August 17, 1969, Camille crashed into the Mississippi coast with sustained winds of 190 to 200 miles (305 to 321 km) an hour and a storm surge of 22 feet (6.7 m).

Scientists at NOAA measure hurricanes by their intensity, or air pressure at the center of the storm. The lower the pressure is, the more intense the hurricane. Here is NOAA's list of the most intense hurricanes to strike the U.S. mainland:

	Name	Category at landfall	Date	Landfall in the U.S.
1	Andrew	Five	August 24, 1992	Southern Florida
2	Camille	Five	August 17, 1969	Mississippi
3	Carla	Five	September 11, 1961	Port O'Connor, Texas
4	Unnamed	Five	September 2, 1935	Florida Keys
5	Donna	Four	September 9, 12, 13, 1960	Florida, North Carolina, and New England
6	Unnamed	Four	September 9, 14, 1919	Florida Keys, Southern Texas
7	Unnamed	Four	September 29, 1915	Grand Isle, Louisiana
8	Unnamed	Four	August 19, 1886	Indianola, Texas
9	Unnamed	Four	August 10, 1856	Last Island, Louisiana
10	Katrina	Three	August 29, 2005	Louisiana, Mississippi

Hurricane Categories

A hurricane is rated on a 1–5 scale based on its severity. The scale, known as the Saffir-Simpson Hurricane Scale, is based on wind speed during a storm and helps scientists estimate the likelihood of property damage and flooding.

Category	Wind Speeds	Damage
1	74–95 mph	minimal
2	96–110 mph	moderate
3	111–130 mph	extensive
4	131–150 mph	extreme
5	155 mph +	catastrophic

Here's something else to think about: global warming changes more than ocean temperatures. It also changes high-level winds and other factors that affect hurricanes. Global warming could actually bring fewer or weaker storms in the future.

Not Enough Information

In the deadliest natural disaster ever to hit the United States, the people of Galveston, Texas, learned firsthand what a hurricane can do. The morning of September 8, 1900, brought black, low-hanging clouds with a few patches of blue sky. A gusty wind kept changing direction, and the sea had already swamped some parts of the city. Local meteorologist Isaac Cline eyed the Gulf of Mexico's brown, foaming swells and worried.

That night, a monster hurricane struck Galveston Island. Wind roared through the city, probably at speeds of about 150 miles (241 km) an hour—there's no way to know for sure, since weather instruments blew apart before the storm peaked. Rising seas crushed buildings near the beach into splinters and bricks. Timbers and trees hurled through the air, smashing everything in their way. A steamship floated out of control on the wild bay, wrecking bridges that connected the island to the mainland.

Through the afternoon and all through the night, the Category Four hurricane pounded Galveston, flooding the entire island. When it was over, more than 8,000 people had died, and most of the city lay in ruin.

Isaac Cline used the best science of his time to track the storm's progress. Still, in 1900, he had no radar or satellite images, no storm-hunting aircraft to go out and measure the hurricane. He didn't know which direction the storm was coming from or where it would strike land. He did issue storm warnings, but never mentioned a hurricane; less than half the people of Galveston left the island. When hurricanes develop today, scientists know more about what they're dealing with.

< The city of Galveston, Texas, destroyed by the hurricane of 1900.

Who Names Hurricanes?

Since 1953, scientists have given names to hurricanes and tropical storms—storms with winds over 39 miles (63 km) an hour. Names allow people to talk about more than one storm without confusion. The World Meteorological Organization (WMO), an international group of weather and climate experts, manages the lists.

For Atlantic hurricanes, the WMO uses six lists of names, one list per year. Names appear on the lists in alphabetical order (*Q, U, X, Y,* and *Z* are not used), alternating between men's and women's names. In the seventh year, the WMO starts over with the first list.

If a storm causes terrible harm, its name is usually crossed off the list, and a new one added. Other parts of the world have different customs for coming up with names. To see if your name is on a list, go to this Web site maintained by NASA: *http://kids.earth.nasa. gov/archive/hurricane/names.html*.

Tracking Hurricane Helene

In early September 2006, a huge storm sprawled over the Atlantic Ocean, just off the coast of Africa. The storm had wallowed in warm water for days, slowly becoming stronger. On the night of September 14, its winds exceeded 39 miles (63 km) an hour, creating Tropical Storm Helene.

The storm moved away from Africa's coast and, by September 16, had a calm eye and stronger winds, with bands of clouds and rain swirling around its center.

From the beginning, researchers scrambled into, above, and around Helene. Satellites took photos and measurements, tracking the storm's course. Storm-hunting P-3 airplanes flew into Helene, and NOAA's G-IV jet flew high around the storm's edges. The crews studied radar and microwave images and dropped miniature weather stations called dropwindsondes into the storm. As they fell, the dropwindsondes recorded information and transmitted it to scientists.

Helene strengthened to a Category Two hurricane, then Category Three, with winds of 121 miles (195 km) an hour. After crossing the tropical Atlantic, Helene began to weaken in cooler waters. Throughout the storm, scientists had detailed information about its strength and location.

Flying into Hurricane Helene, scientists gained knowledge that may help them understand the birth of hurricanes. As they learn how storms will behave on a warmer planet, they may learn to predict entire seasons of hurricanes. Meteorologists may soon be able to warn fishers in Florida and New England when a busy hurricane season is on its way or advise Indonesian farmers when a season will not bring the heavy rains they hope for. Weather science is not there yet, but scientists have taken on the challenge.

Meet a Meteorologist

Dr. Robert Rogers is a meteorologist with the National Oceanic and Atmospheric Administration. He researches hurricanes, using complex computer models and observations collected from aircraft and satellites.

Q: What is an average day at your job like?

A: That depends on what time of year it is. For most of the year, I am working in my office, running and analyzing computer simulations of hurricanes, analyzing observations of hurricanes, writing and reviewing papers to scientific journals, and preparing and giving talks and seminars at various meetings.

During the hurricane season, I sometimes get the opportunity to fly into hurricanes. We take measurements in these storms to provide observations for the forecasters at the National Hurricane Center and also to analyze later to improve our understanding of how hurricanes work.

Q: What type of plane do you fly on, and what is your job when you are in the air?

A: I fly primarily on a plane called the P-3. It is a propeller-driven plane with four engines. It's mostly used in the U.S. Navy to fly at very low altitudes over the ocean looking for submarines. The P-3s I fly on have been modified to fly into hurricanes. That includes a hardened frame, plus instruments like radar on the plane and chutes for dropping probes into the air below the aircraft.

When I am on the plane, I can do a variety of jobs. These include overseeing the scientific activities on the plane . . . and monitoring [equipment].

Q: How far from or into storms do you fly?

A: On the P-3s we fly right into the heart of the storm. We often are tasked with finding the center of the storm to relay information on the exact location and intensity of the storm back to the National Hurricane Center. We fly into the core of the storm at altitudes usually ranging between

∧ A P-3 airplane, outfitted with a circular "eye" on the bottom of the aircraft, flies into the eye of Hurricane Caroline, which struck Brownsville, Texas, in 1975.

5,000 [1525 m] and 15,000 feet [4575 m].

Once you're in the storm, it can definitely be exciting. [On a flight into a 2005 hurricane], I was strapped in, but I had a clipboard and a can of soda that [were] not. When we hit the turbulence, I had to catch my soda can and clipboard, because they were hovering around my face!

▣: Who is on the airplane with you when you fly into a storm?

▣: There are usually 15 to 18 people on the plane when we fly into the storm. These include the flight crew—pilots, flight director, navigator, flight engineer, and instrument engineers—as well as scientific crew. I am part of the scientific crew, which is usually between two and five people.

▣: What qualifications would a person need to do the kind of work that you do?

▣: Generally people who do what I do have gone to school for a long time. . . . You don't need a Ph.D. to study hurricanes, but you definitely need to be good in math and science. And above all, you need a passion for learning.

▣: Is there anything else you would like us to know?

▣: While hurricanes can be very destructive and deadly, they also play a vital role in the Earth's climate, transporting heat from the warm oceans to the atmosphere and toward the polar regions. Some parts of the world depend on the rainfall from hurricanes for their annual rainfall totals.

So if we could somehow eliminate hurricanes from existence, it would certainly be valuable as far as reducing death and destruction along the coastlines. But it would also have negative consequences that we may not be thinking about as much.

Collecting Dust

CHAPTER 5

Saharan Dust Clouds Streak Across the Atlantic

E very summer, great clouds of reddish-gold dust swirl up from Africa's Sahara Desert, rising 3 and 4 miles (4.8 and 6.4 km) into the sky. Powerful winds carry the dust out over the Atlantic Ocean, where it blasts through storms along Africa's coast, dropping fine particles into the water along the way. Tiny ocean plants called phytoplankton soak up the dust, hungry for the iron and other minerals it contains.

Thousands of miles across the sea, the dust smudges Caribbean skies with brown haze. In Central America and Texas, it sets off coughing

< Dust storms in African deserts send millions of tons of dust into the air. The dust eventually settles in the Atlantic Ocean, warming the waters and affecting the development of hurricanes throughout the world.

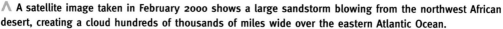

∧ A satellite image taken in February 2000 shows a large sandstorm blowing from the northwest African desert, creating a cloud hundreds of thousands of miles wide over the eastern Atlantic Ocean.

spells and burning eyes, and in Florida, dirty raindrops leave reddish spots on cars. It's uncomfortable and inconvenient—but there may be good news about dust.

In Dakar, capital city of the African nation of Senegal, scientists wake up at 5 a.m. to prepare for a day of chasing dust. After a quick breakfast they climb aboard a storm-hunting jet to track great clouds of dust blown off the Sahara. They sweat beneath their flight suits—it's hot on the plane. The jet zooms back and forth through brown and gold skies—above, into, and below the clouds—taking air samples at different altitudes. It makes a steep turn, and everyone holds on tight, feeling sick. Working at a frenzied pace, scientists check instruments, measure how much sunlight the dust reflects into space, and collect sample after sample. Later, in the laboratory, they pore over the samples to discover what minerals they contain.

A few hundred miles away, a second team of scientists fight seasickness aboard a research ship in the rolling Atlantic. After a while, churning stomachs settle, and the ship's laboratories fill up with scientists getting to work. They have learned to tie everything down, because if they don't, equipment bounces across the floor with every swell. On a zigzagging course, the ship drops large bottles connected to lines into the waves to collect water samples. The researchers analyze minerals in the samples and study phytoplankton. The scientists want to know where dust settles out of the sky and what happens when it lands in the ocean.

The goal of both groups is to learn how dust blown off the Sahara affects our climate and our oceans.

Dust May Be a Good Thing

More than 170 years ago, scientist Charles Darwin noted African dust settling over the ship he was traveling with, H.M.S. *Beagle.* In fact, the reddish clouds would be hard to miss—they carry millions of tons of dust across the ocean.

Along the way, that dust may be doing some good. Thunderstorms in the Cape Verde region off the western coast of Africa often grow up to be Atlantic hurricanes. Saharan dust saps the strength from the storms, so that they never become hurricanes. One reason dust is thought to weaken hurricanes is that the dust reflects sunlight, preventing it from warming the ocean surface. (A warm ocean is a necessary ingredient for hurricanes.)

Charles Darwin

There may also be a connection between Saharan dust and climate change. The dust is full of minerals that certain ocean plants, including phytoplankton, need in order to grow. Out in the middle of the Atlantic, dust clouds are one of the few sources these plants have for nutrients. So falling dust acts like fertilizer, and the phytoplankton hit a growth spurt. When plants grow, they soak up carbon dioxide (a greenhouse gas) from the atmosphere. When they die, they sink deep into the ocean, taking some of the carbon with them, safely away from Earth's atmosphere, for thousands of years.

Dust and the Amazon Rain Forest

The same dust clouds that sprinkle nutrient-rich particles over the Atlantic Ocean blow all the way to South America's Amazon River Basin. There, too, Saharan dust settles out of the sky, showering the canopy of the rain forest with iron and other minerals. The rain forest needs this "free meal" from the sky because frequent, heavy rains wash minerals out of the soil. Without Saharan dust, the lush trees and vines of the rain forest might not survive. Plants of the rain forest soak up carbon dioxide, reducing greenhouse gases in Earth's atmosphere.

The Amazon rain forest is a big help in the fight against global warming. Not only does it take carbon

< Scientists studying rainfall in the Amazon come into contact with animals like these jaguar cubs.

dioxide out of the air as it grows, but it may actually grow more when carbon dioxide is increased. Since carbon dioxide is a greenhouse gas that encourages global warming, the rain forest may work hardest against global warming when its help is most needed. Unfortunately, we are helping to destroy the rain forest that helps us fight global warming. Each year, farmers and road builders clear an area of rain forest larger

How Much Rain Does a Rain Forest Need?

When the rain forest is dry, the tallest trees drop foliage and die back, spilling sunlight on the forest floor. Grasses spring up amid the carpet of dead leaves—perfect kindling for accidental fires. Scientists say that drought and fire may be the greatest threats facing the Amazon rain forest.

There was a time when the Amazon rain forest was threatened by natural fires once every few centuries. Now, global warming and frequent El Niños bring drought (and drought-related fires) to the Amazon Basin every few years.

Researchers from the Woods Hole Research Center decided to deliberately create

a drought in one small part of the rain forest in order to see for themselves how the forest responds. During the Amazon's rainy season, they used plastic panels to block rain from reaching the ground. Rainwater ran off the panels into plastic-lined trenches that carried it away. The scientists dug deep pits and lined them with wood, so that they could climb down to see how much water the soil held.

All this digging brought out some curious neighbors. Caimans (smaller cousins of alligators) watched slyly from muddy pools in the road. Trenches running with rainwater drew snakes,

including great, muscled boa constrictors. Workers dumping out full wheelbarrows found themselves eye-to-eye with jaguars sitting atop their dirt pile.

When the rainy season ended, researchers removed the panels and watched the forest closely. Satellite images provided by NASA showed trees becoming less green—the soil didn't hold enough moisture to support them through the dry season. Tall, fast-growing trees fell, letting harsh, tropical sunlight dry the forest floor. Smaller plants weakened, dropping leaves and increasing the danger of fire.

∧ Fire rages in the distance of this area of Brazilian rain forest, where residents regularly burn the forest to clear land for grazing cattle. Land belonging to the forest-dwelling Yanomami tribe is also regularly threatened.

than Massachusetts. Scientists and governments wrestle with this problem, because many of those clearing the trees are local people, earning their living. The question is how to stop the clearing without creating problems for people who live and work in the region.

The rain forest ecosystem is one of the richest in the world. Thirty million people live there, alongside at least one-fourth of Earth's species. Many of these plants and animals could become extinct if the rain forest can't be saved.

Answers Lead to More Questions

On a long flight over the desert, dust-chasing pilots point out camels plodding across the sand below. It's been a busy, exhausting day for the scientists. They look over measurements that tell them how much light the dust storm reflected into space. This is another important part of dust science, because large, dense clouds can block the sun completely, cooling oceans and land beneath. Will the reflected heat be enough to counteract global warming? Probably not, but what will happen if the Sahara Desert grows, kicking up even more dust?

Scientists say that in Earth's past cold periods, deserts across the planet grew and produced more dust. Did this extra dust help *make* the planet cold? Could Saharan dust be part of Earth's built-in response to global warming—a sort of self-healing process? Where global warming is concerned, every answer that scientists find brings a whole new set of questions.

Forecast for the Future

Signs of a Changing World

For 50 years, from 1950 to 2005, stonemason Edward Gange roamed the countryside of Salisbury, England, searching for mushrooms. Whenever he saw something interesting, he wrote down a description of it. Gange's friends joined in the hunt, bringing him samples of mushrooms they'd spotted and thought he might like. Over time, he put together quite a record of how mushrooms grew in Salisbury; in fact, he had 52,000 sightings.

Gange's mushroom hunting might have remained just an unusual hobby if his son had not become an

< The fluted white Helvella mushroom is common in North America. Global warming may increase the times of the year when the mushrooms thrive.

ecologist at the University of London. Young Alan Gange studied his father's mushroom records and came up with startling conclusions. Edward had recorded seeing many of the same kinds of mushrooms at the same time year after year. In recent years, they've begun popping up at different times of the year. As many as one-third now bear fruit twice in a year, instead of once. The mushrooms, which thrive in a warm, damp environment, are changing along with Earth's climate.

∧ Alan Gange, son of Edward Gange

More Than Mushrooms

Mushrooms are only one sign that Earth's climate is changing. Here are a few other examples:

▦ One hundred years ago, Alaska's Icy Bay was all ice, no bay. Now, glaciers are melting so fast you can literally see it happen, and Icy Bay is full of water.

▦ Colorado's pikas—busy creatures that look a little like prairie dogs—are moving higher into the Rocky Mountains. Once so common on lower slopes that many people considered them pests, the tiny pikas now live mainly at higher, cooler elevations.

∧ A Colorado pika

▦ In Boston, some mosquitoes have evolved to go into hibernation more than a week later than they did 30 years ago. This means that their internal clock has changed, telling them it's safe to stay out for a week longer. Why? Because the weather stays warm longer than it once did. Only a handful of animals have evolved (physically changed from generation to generation) to survive global warming.

▦ Researchers found 5,000-year-old plants around the edges of a melting glacier in Peru. Because the plants are not fossilized or decayed, researchers believe they've been covered with ice since the glacier formed. This would mean that the area's climate changed suddenly enough to freeze the plants and has not been as warm as it is now for the last 50 centuries.

▦ Icy lakes in northern New England thaw eight days earlier than they did forty years ago.

The United Kingdom—all of Europe, for that matter—is quite a bit hotter than it was fifty years ago. In the summer of 2003, London was so hot that zookeepers in the London Zoo fed giant popsicles to tigers to help them cool off. In other parts of the U.K., trains had to slow down because officials worried that rails might buckle in the heat. Temperatures rose above 100°F (38°C), far hotter than usual.

Across Europe, that summer was a scorcher. In Paris, France, children waded in the city's famous fountains to get cool. Power plants overheated and shut down, leaving large parts of the city without electricity. Many people became sick from the heat, and some died. Even the snowy mountains of Switzerland felt the heat wave. Long-frozen ground on the Matterhorn, a high peak in the Alps, thawed and broke apart. Forty mountain climbers had to be rescued, and the mountain was closed to climbers for a week.

Summer heat waves continue to plague Europe, but in a strange twist, some scientists think global warming could push the climate in the opposite direction.

▼ Children play in the Trocadero Fountains in Paris, France, during the summer of 2003. Unusually high temperatures throughout Europe are thought to be a result of global warming.

The Other Extreme

If you were to make a map of what global warming might bring to various parts of Earth, you'd have to draw a big question mark over the North Atlantic Ocean and, for that matter, much of the Northern Hemisphere. Will it grow hotter? Will it grow colder? No one knows, because we don't know enough about how oceans affect our climate.

Here's what we do know: Water in the world's oceans flows in a large belt-like path that encircles the planet. In the North Atlantic, warm water near the surface flows north, cooling as it goes. Scientists think this warm water helps keep weather mild in Europe and the northeastern United States. As it moves toward the Arctic, the water grows cold enough to sink (cold water is denser than warm). The deep, cold water flows south again in a path sometimes called the ocean conveyor belt.

What we don't know: how might global warming change that current? As glaciers and ice sheets melt, they dump fresh water into the ocean conveyor belt. Cold, fresh water sinks more slowly than saltwater. Could too much fresh water cause the North Atlantic conveyor belt to slow down or even stop? If the conveyor belt stops, Europe and the northeastern U.S. could get chilly in a hurry.

▽ The ocean-circulation pattern known as the ocean conveyor belt provides nutrients for sea life around the world.

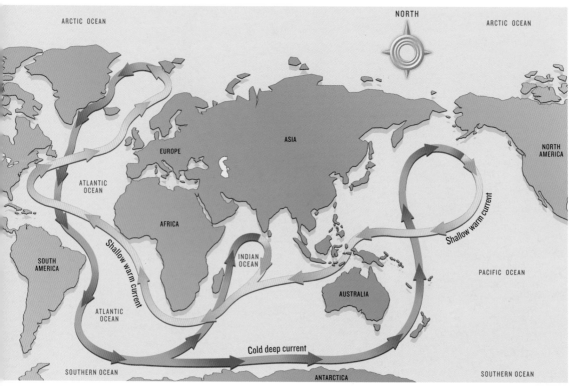

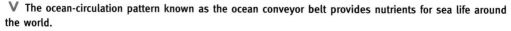

A Glimpse of the Future?

Americans living in northeastern states have plenty of experience with snow and ice. February 2007 offered a sample of how fierce winter could be. Some parts of New York State received 10 feet (3 m) of the white stuff in the first weeks of February. Then, on Valentine's Day, a snowstorm blew across the Midwest and up the Atlantic coastline into Canada, burying a good part of the U.S. in snow and ice.

Roads closed, and banks of snow drifted higher and higher, burying cars and trucks. At airports in New York, jets loaded with passengers sat frozen on runways for hours. Many airports closed. Schools and universities closed, too, but children weren't running around pitching snowballs and making snow angels—almost no one ventured outside. A thick, slippery layer of ice coated everything in sight. Power lines came crashing down, and more than 300,000 people were left without electricity. They hunkered down wherever they could, longing for spring.

⋀ The Valentine's Day storm of February 2007 covered most of the country in snow and ice.

Blizzards—The Worst and the Whitest

According to the National Weather Service, a storm becomes a blizzard when wind, mixed with snow, blows at least 35 miles (56 km) an hour and temperatures fall to 20°F (minus 7°C).

■ The storm that blasted the northern Great Plains in January 1888 will forever be known as the Schoolchildren's Blizzard. On the morning of January 12, temperatures were mild, but before school let out that afternoon, the weather suddenly changed. Snow blew so thick people couldn't tell Earth from sky, and children were trapped in one-room schoolhouses, with no way to go home. Many of those who tried were lost in the storm and died.

■ The Great White "Hurricane" of March 1888 sank 200 ships up and down the East Coast, from Maryland to Canada. The city of New York lay paralyzed by the blizzard. In some parts of the Northeast, snowdrifts stood 50 feet (15 m) high. More than 400 people died in this storm.

■ In 1949, a November blizzard pounded Nebraska and marooned

On February 6, 1978, hurricane-strength winds hit the northeastern U.S., pushing a wall of white cold across cities and farms. In an area already blanketed with 2 feet (0.6 m) of snow, the blizzard dumped another 4 feet (1.2 m) of the white stuff. People who stepped outside in the whiteout conditions became lost just a few feet from their doors.

In January 1996, a blizzard held the U.S. prisoner, from parts of the

∧ A blizzard in 1888 covered the streets of New York with 40 inches of snow, downing telegraph and telephone poles and paralyzing the city with winds of 60 mph and snow drifts 50 feet high.

∧ Vehicles were abandoned all along the highway in Dedham, Massachusetts, after the blizzard of February 1978. Cars and trucks had to be dug out with plows days later.

Wyoming drivers in their cars. Banks of snow buried cars and roads; schools and businesses were forced to close. In January 1950, another blizzard blew down from Canada, invading Wyoming, the Dakotas, Nebraska, Kansas, and Colorado. The snow drifted so high so fast that it stopped trains. When the snow and wind eased, Air Force planes dropped supplies to people stuck in remote areas, along with more than a thousand tons of hay for hungry cattle.

West and Midwest to the East Coast. Some areas received over 2 feet (0.6 m) of snow, which melted in the warm days that immediately followed, bringing devastating floods.

The Valentine's Day Blizzard of 2007 crushed towns, farms, and cities from Nebraska to Massachusetts. People were stranded in cars, restaurants, and offices. Hundreds of thousands lost electricity. Across the country, airplanes sat on runways waiting to be de-iced as stranded travelers slept in airports for days.

Icy, cold weather is nothing new. The North Atlantic has seen cooling periods before—the last one began about 1300 and lasted more than 500 years. Europe's glaciers spread, invading farmland and even villages.

People had to leave their homes or starve. At one point, New York Harbor froze over, and people walked across it from Manhattan to Staten Island. Some other regions suffered icy conditions as well.

This kind of cooling doesn't happen in a few days, but it can happen quickly. In the past, Earth's climate has sometimes changed dramatically in less than a decade.

▼ **Children sled down the Capitol Building steps covered in snow during a January 1996 snowstorm that dropped over two feet of snow in some areas.**

The Years Ahead

∧ The director of the National Hurricane Center, Max Mayfield, watches satellite images of Tropical Storm Ernesto hitting the shores of southern Florida in August 2006.

Today, supercomputers run modeling programs that paint a detailed picture of what Earth was like thousands of years ago. Unmanned aircraft called aerosondes fly into storms too dangerous for researchers to observe firsthand, taking precise measurements and transmitting them to scientists. Satellites measure everything from the size of tropical ice caps to the amount of moisture in the ground. With this information, scientists can tell how fast glaciers are melting and where flooding will result if more rain falls. Drilling ice cores gives us a history of climate change so we can better manage the conditions occurring now. Scientists all over the planet brave extreme weather conditions to bring new information to light. With increased knowledge and commitment it is hoped we can slow the pace of global warming.

Glossary

atmosphere — layers of gases that surround Earth

buoy — floating object placed in a lake, river, or ocean to serve a specific purpose, such as holding weather instruments

current — the flow of a body of gas or liquid

drought — an extended period of dry weather

ecosystem — a system formed by the interaction of a community of living things and their environment

Equator — an imaginary line that runs east and west around the middle of Earth

evaporate — to change from a liquid to a gas

expand — to become larger

forecast — to describe in advance what will happen

heat wave — a short period of extremely hot weather

hemisphere — either half of earth as divided by the Equator

meteorologist — a scientist who studies weather

paleoclimatologist —a scientist who studies climate by researching the past

radar — an instrument that uses radio waves to find and measure distant objects

satellite — any object or instrument that orbits a planet

stalactite — a mineral deposit in the shape of an icicle hanging from the roof of a cave

stalagmite — a mineral deposit in the shape of an icicle jutting upward from the floor of a cave

technology — science; use of scientific knowledge

tropical — having to do with warm areas of Earth near the Equator

◁ The sulfur tuft is a poisonous mushroom found in the Northern Hemisphere. Blooms of the specimen have been occurring as late as December due to warmer temperatures throughout the region.

Bibliography

Books

Burt, Christopher C. *Extreme Weather.* New York: W. W. Norton, 2007.

Henson, Robert. *The Rough Guide to Climate Change.* 2nd Edition. New York: Rough Guides, 2008.

Larson, Erik. *Isaac's Storm.* New York: Random House, 1999.

Articles

Gaines, Ernest J. "New Orleans, Home No More." NATIONAL GEOGRAPHIC (August 2006): 42-65.

On the Web

National Aeronautics and Space Administration
http://www.nasa.gov/worldbook/weather_worldbook.html

National Oceanographic and Atmospheric Administration
http://www.noaa.gov/

National Weather Service
http://www.weather.gov/om/reachout/winter.shtml

Weatherwise
http://www.nasa.bbc.co.uk/weather/weatherwise/index.shtml

Further Reading

Aquado, Edward and James Burt. *Understanding Weather and Climate.* New Jersey: Prentice Hall, 2006.

Charlevoix, Donna, Bob Rauber, and John Walsh. *Severe and Hazardous Weather: An Introduction to High Impact Meteorology.* Dubuque, Iowa: Kendall Hunt, 2005.

Kahl, Jonathan. *National Audubon Society First Field Guide to Weather.* New York: Scholastic, 1998.

Tocci, Salvatore. *Experiments With Weather.* Connecticut: Children's Press, 2004.

Weather (DK Guide). New York: Dorling Kindersley, 2006.

Λ A man carries his child to safety amid rising floodwaters near Quezon City in the Philippines during May 1997. El Niño probably contributed to the damaging rains that washed away towns in this island city.

Index

Boldface indicates illustrations.

About the Author

A storm-lover from childhood, Kathleen Simpson has experienced extreme weather first-hand, from drought and heat of 112°F to a Category Two hurricane. The awful beauty of lightning, treetops bending in the wind, and heavy, rolling thunderheads still brings her out onto the porch to weather-watch. Ms. Simpson lives in the hill country of Central Texas with her two children, husband, and dogs. She has authored five books for young people. *National Geographic Investigates Extreme Weather* is the first book she has written for the Society.

About the Consultant

After receiving his Ph.D. from the University of Michigan, Dr. Jonathan Kahl joined a team of NOAA scientists studying Arctic weather and air pollution. His research has included studies of Grand Canyon haze, Hawaiian winds, and acid rain in Central America. His most exciting moments have included shivering through –30°C (–22°F) Siberian temperatures and narrowly escaping Hurricane Wilma in Cancun, Mexico. Dr. Kahl teaches meteorology at the University of Wisconsin-Milwaukee.

∧ The United Nations Conference on Climate Change in Montreal in 2005 attracted people calling for government action to reduce greenhouse gases in response to global warming.

Founded in 1888, the National Geographic Society is one of the largest nonprofit scientific and educational organizations in the world. It reaches more than 285 million people worldwide each month through its official journal, NATIONAL GEOGRAPHIC, and its four other magazines; the National Geographic Channel; television documentaries; radio programs; films; books; videos and DVDs; maps; and interactive media. National Geographic has funded more than 8,000 scientific research projects and supports an education program combating geographic illiteracy.

For more information, please call 1-800-NGS LINE (647-5463) or write to the following address:

National Geographic Society
1145 17th Street N.W., Washington, D.C.
20036-4688 U.S.A.

Visit us online at
www.nationalgeographic.com/books

For librarians and teachers:
www.ngchildrensbooks.com

More for kids from National Geographic:
kids.nationalgeographic.com

For information about special discounts for bulk purchases, please contact National Geographic Books Special Sales: ngspecsales@ngs.org

For rights or permissions inquiries, please contact National Geographic Books Subsidiary Rights: ngbookrights@ngs.org

Library of Congress Cataloging-in-Publication Data available upon request

Hardcover ISBN: 978-1-4263-0359-3
Library ISBN: 978-1-4263-0281-7

Printed in China

Book design by Dan Banks, Project Design Company

Published by the
National Geographic Society
John M. Fahey, Jr., *President and Chief Executive Officer;* Gilbert M. Grosvenor, *Chairman of the Board;* Tim T. Kelly, *President, Global Media Group;* Nina D. Hoffman, *Executive Vice President; President, Book Publishing Group*

Prepared by the Book Division
Nancy Laties Feresten, *Vice President, Editor in Chief, Children's Books*
Bea Jackson, *Director of Design and Illustrations, Children's Books*
Amy Shields, *Executive Editor, Series, Children's Books*
Carl Mehler, *Director of Maps*

Staff for This Book
Virginia Ann Koeth, *Editor*
Jim Hiscott, *Art Director*
Lori Epstein, *Illustrations Editor*
Lewis R. Bassford, *Production Manager*
Grace Hill, *Associate Managing Editor*
Stuart Armstrong, *Graphics*
Jennifer A. Thornton, *Managing Editor*
R. Gary Colbert, *Production Director*
Susan Borke, *Legal and Business Affairs*

Manufacturing and Quality Management
Christopher A. Liedel, *Chief Financial Officer*
Phillip L. Schlosser, *Vice President*
Chris Brown, *Technical Director*
Nicole Elliott, *Manager*

Photo Credits
Front cover: Jessica Rinaldi/ Reuters/ Corbis
Back & Spine: Mehau Kulyk/ Photo Researchers, Inc.
Back Icon: Christoper Mampe/ Shutterstock

AP = Associated Press; 1, AP; 2-3, OAR/ERL/National Severe Storms Laboratory (NSSL); 4, AP; 6, Jeff Schmaltz, MODIS Rapid Response Team, NASA/GSFC; 8, courtesy of the consultant; 9, Giraud Philippe/ Corbis Sygma; 10, NOAA's National Weather Service (NWS) Collection; 10, AP; 11, Michael Van Woert, NOAA NESDIS, ORA; 11, 12-13, 14, AP; 15 top, Peter Sloss NOAA/NGDC; 15 bottom, National Oceanic and Atmospheric Administration Paleoclimatology Program/Department of Commerce Lonnie Thompson Byrd Polar Research Center, The Ohio State University; 16, Dianne Winter/Andrill; 17 top, AP; 17 bottom, AP; 19, 20-21, AP; 22 top Jack Atley/Bloomberg News/Landov; 22 bottom, AP; 22 AP; 23, Reuters/luis Galdamez /Landov; 24, Courtesy of Janece McDonald; 25, NOAA Photo Library, Historic NWS collection; 26 top, AP; 26 bottom, NOAA's National Weather Service (NWS) Collection; 27, AP; 28-29, © Sean Ramsay/Image Works; 30 top, AP; bottom, AP; 32, NASA/NASDA; 33, NOAA / PMEL / TAO Project Office, Dr. Michael J. McPhaden, Director; 34, Courtesy NASA/JPL-Caltech; 35, AP; 36-37, NASA; 38, 40, AP; 42, 43, NOAA; 44-45, Peter Chadwick/Photo Researchers, Inc.; 46, NASA; 47, 48, 49, AP; 50-51, 52, Courtesy of Alan Gange; 52, Photos.com; 53, AP; 55, 56 top and bottom, 57, 58, AP; 59, Courtesy of Alan Gange; 60, 63, AP

Front cover: A man digs out after a blizzard hit the Boston area in January, 2005.

Back cover: Hurricane evacuation sign

Page 1: Once a reservoir where residents enjoyed outdoor activities, Pejar Dam in Goulburn, Australia, was all but dried up in 2005, the hottest year on record in one of the driest countries on Earth.

Pages 2–3: This tornado formed in May 1999 near Oklahoma City, Oklahoma.

A Creative Media Applications, Inc. Production
Editor: Susan Madoff
Copy Editor: Laurie Lieb
Design and Production: Luís Leon and Fabia Wargin